Real
Women

Don't Wear Pants!

From the Series:
5 Things Real Women Don't Do

By Charlette Williams

A MissCharlette Publication
CreateSpace
ISBN –13: 978-1466262669
ISBN –10: 1466262664

YOUR THOUGHTS BECOME
YOUR DESTINY

Watch your thoughts;
they become words.

Watch your words;
they become actions.

Watch your actions;
they become habits.

Watch your habits;
they become character.

Watch your character;
for it becomes your destiny.

- *Unknown*

TABLE OF CONTENTS

Chapter 1

Real Women Don't Wear Pants!

Well ok . . . that's just my personal soap box. Meaning, since we *are* women, shouldn't we look like women. The true title includes the word "*the.*" *Real Women Don't Wear **The** Pants!* Unless, of course she's ok with never having true happiness, the man of her dreams, contentment, and all the other benefits of a wonderfully fulfilled life that today's woman claims to be striving for.

Or is that really what women are striving for? If so, most are going about it the wrong way. In fact, the path that most women are on today will bring them the exact opposite: unhappiness, Mr. Wrong (*if not manless altogether*), discontentment and a guaranteed unfulfilled life.

So what is it that today's women are doing that is so wrong?

Well, pretty much everything from raising children alone, having careers, pursuing men and of course, **wearing the pants**. I realize these are blunt statements, but there is no need to sugar coat the facts.

The *Real Women Don't* series came about to address questions I hear time and time again from women everywhere. You know the ones like: "Where are all the good men?" "Why do men cheat?" And on and on and blah, blah, blah . . . I'll tell you why, but you're not going to like it. Fortunately, the series is not about me making new friends.

8

Ok, back to those questions. The one I hear the most and for which the answer is as plain as day, yet women can't see it is:

Why am I still single?

"I'm a good woman".

"I have a lot going for myself".

"I make my own money".

"I bought my own house"

"I have degrees, a great career".

"I'm a great catch".

So why am I still single?

Wow...All nice attributes to bring to the table and you *are* a good catch—for someone who values those attributes, or someone who thinks the same as you do.

So yes, you would be a ***great*** catch . . .

. . . *for a woman!!!*

You see, women think those things are good to bring to the table; men don't. Women think so because those are the attributes *they* want from a potential mate. Men want something very different from a potential mate.

What's so puzzling is why smart, intelligent women of the 21st Century can't comprehend this concept. The concept that men and women are different. We know that men and women are different, right? We know that men don't think like us and we don't think like them, right? Is it that we just don't believe it? We've heard it over and over, time and time again. So why are we so perplexed when men aren't *falling at our feet* and *chasing us down* but instead, running from us. Because they don't care that we got all that 'going on'. Why?

Because Ladies . . .

***We've got the wrong things
going on at the wrong time!***

So . . . we can keep being
appealing to *women* . . . **or** we can
start becoming more appealing to
men. It really is that simple!

Now I can just hear you saying,
"Not all men feel that way." Well
. . . yes . . . all men do! But let
me be clear – when I say men, I
mean real men! Not little boys
who haven't grown up yet; not
players who have something to
prove; not liars, cheaters, addicts,
etc.

These are all characteristics of a
male who is broken, who has
issues, who is immature-- or
maybe a generally good guy who
is still evolving into a *real* man.

Real men naturally respect
women, pursue women, protect
women, lead women, and take
care of women. Real men are
chivalrous. They are gentlemen,
conquerors and leaders.

So, when I hear things like "my man likes the fact that I'm a strong, independent, self-sufficient, opinionated woman," just remember, were talking apples and oranges here, "your" man is a male whose characteristics derive from what today's society has taught him to be. The man I'm talking about is a man whose characteristics derive from his creator's original instructions on manhood.

RED ALERT...RED ALERT!

Beware the following:

-If your man *expects*, *insists*, or *wants*, you to go to work daily as he does so that you can help pay your share of the household bills;

-If your man wants to stay home and be "Mr. Mom" while you go to work every day;

-If your man is ok with you wearing the pants in the family;

-If your man insist on going dutch during the dating stage of the relationship;

-If your man is ok with pre-marital sex with *you;* then . . .

YOU'VE GOT THE WRONG MAN!!!

Because somewhere down the line, once you discover the role of a *real* man, you're going to become resentful of him, have no respect for him, withdraw yourself from him, and eventually, well . . . we know where this is going.

I know, I know, I can hear you saying, "but I didn't know he was like that when I chose him." To that I say-- that statement is just wrong – on so many levels. First of all, real women don't choose men. They don't chase, find, pursue, or otherwise choose men (more on that later in the series, see *Real Women Don't Pursue Men*).

Then there's the whole *"I didn't know"* defense. Ladies! Please! We are really going to have to come up with something better than this. This defense is just not believable-- not by me, not by you and especially not by the guy or guys who have mistreated you. Which, by the way, is exactly the reason you've been mistreated in the first place. These guys believe you are very aware of their intentions because they're not hiding them, and you're accepting them.

If you are exhibiting certain behaviors, a real man won't even look your way when he is in serious pursuit of a mate. Why? Because real men have clear radar on women with *no standards*, and he *will* steer clear. On the other hand, when guys know that you will accept anything, they will gladly mess around with you, kick it with you, even play house with you but they usually have no intentions of *growing up for you, cleaning up their act*, or *taking you seriously*. And it doesn't matter what you do. You won't change his mind or his intentions toward you. That doesn't make him a bad person or a 'dog.' He just hasn't had an incentive to be a real man to you. Only a real woman inspires that kind of change.

Remember, men are wired and designed in a way that they either really want you or they don't. There's no rhyme or reason to this. If a man is attracted to you, smitten with you and **really** wants you, he will move *heaven & earth* to get what he **really** wants. And you don't have to do anything – except be womanly. You don't have to strategically place yourself in the right place at the right time in order to be *noticed* by Mr. Right. Mr. Right <u>will</u> <u>find</u> <u>you</u> *if* he **really** wants you.

If, on the other hand, he doesn't **really** want you, then *–and I know this may be hard to believe*—but he just may not be that into you. Oh he might still mess around with you, but he won't have that *thing* for you that causes him to pursue you at all cost. That's not to say that he won't jump through a few hoops for you. After all, he does still like sex and will sometimes go out of his way and do things he wouldn't otherwise do to get it. Don't make the mistake of thinking he did it because you're so special to him. Let's be clear, his motive is sex. And we can't blame him for being who he naturally is. The signs of a man's intentions towards you are always there if you just take the time to look. Most guys are not very good at pretending to be someone they're not. The ones who are usually don't have the capacity or the incentive to keep up the pretense for any extended period of time. This is another reason to just give yourself time.

Eventually, he will reveal who he is and it really won't take very long.

Genuine people in general are naturally an open book. This is especially true for most men. So Ladies, we can't continue to say we didn't know who he was until after we gave him our heart (and by heart, we mean sex). Once again, that's on us, Ladies. Usually, it's not that we didn't know . . . it's that we didn't *want* to know. We didn't take the time to know. We purposely didn't see or didn't learn from what we saw. We told ourselves he was one thing, when all the signs pointed to him being something else. We believed about him what we wanted to believe, despite all indications to the contrary.

This brings us to the real reason women should never pursue men – not in any way, shape or form. And the reason I say "real women" never do. You see, to pursue men is to set yourself up for a lifetime of relationship disasters. We weren't designed to take on this task. Remember, men and women were designed differently and men were wired specifically to take on the task of pursuit. Here is a quote that reflects that fact:

"Women fall in love and get married. Men decide to get married, then look for a wife."
[Author unknown]

Think about it Ladies…this explains why so many women are crushed when: she finds the guy of her dreams, puts everything she has into the relationship for years and things are good, except, *he- just- won't –marry- her.* She finally gives him the ultimatum, *"marry me or it's over".* He chooses *"over".* They go their separate ways. Then, a short time later, to her disbelief, she finds out that he married the very next woman he became involved with.

It really isn't a mystery Ladies; men just don't think like us.

Remember when we talked about how men either love you or they don't? No rhyme or reason?

Well, women on the other hand, are the opposite. Even though we try to fight it *tooth and nail*. We were designed to be and are naturally nurturing creatures. If we are treated well, protected, pampered, taken care of and made to feel special; our heart goes completely out of our control and straight to the one who makes us feel so special, protected and loved. You see, the way we're wired, we learn to love … men don't. Our minds will change about what we want. A man's won't. This is why I often say a man can have any women he wants. Very few believe this – even men, and especially women – but it's true.

19

If it sounds like I'm on the *man's* side or that I'm rooting for them to win this everlasting battle between the sexes, it's because… *I am!* But, what that really means is, I'm rooting for *women*. I'm rooting for women everywhere to have true happiness, a fulfilled life and sweet contentment. So yes, I want men to win because when they win, we win! We're not going to change them or beat them at their own game Ladies, so we might as well join them-- support them-- submit to them-- and be lead by them. When men thrive, women are the real winners.

Now that we've broken the ice Ladies, let me just reiterate that I *am* on our side, I *am* rooting for us, for our happiness and for a fulfilled life. Although it may not sound like it as you continue reading, it's true. It's the reason I am writing this series of books in the first place – I want us all to win. Men and women.

Now I am very aware that what I express in this series will not be very popular – truth never is. In fact, most of what I say here will be flat-out rejected by most of today's modern women because it requires a significant change of mindset and *life principles*. It will be especially hard for those hearing it for the first time. But the reason I continue is that I know, depending on where you are in *your* life, you will either *hear me now* or *hear me later*. The fact is, *the truth is the truth-- is the truth.* It doesn't change because we want it to, or because women's lib says so, or because it's the 21st century. Some of us may have an "aha moment", while others will need to hear it several times in several ways, from several people and even then, only a seed will be planted. The point is, sooner or later we women are going to have to face cold hard facts. And the fact is:

21

It's a Man's World and we were created _from_ him -- _for him_. There! I said it. It's their world Ladies and we were designed and given to them for the purpose of *assisting* them as they rule their world. Yes I said that too. Men Rule the world, they always have and they always will . . . period. It is as simple as that. That's the way it was meant to be and we're not going to change it no matter how much we "bring home the bacon and fry it up in the pan." We can continue to try to change things, and do things *our* way but let's face it Ladies, we are the special order item, created and designed just for them. Meaning, we are second to them –naturally-- and the natural order of things *will* prevail. To deny it is simply going against the natural grain. We can try until the end of time, but if we do, we will continue down the path of unhappiness, unfulfillment and discontent until the end of time also.

Now I know what you're
thinking: "How can that be?"
"We have evolved." "That kind
of thinking will only set us back."
"That's old fashioned." "No one
thinks like that anymore." Yes—
yes, I've heard it all. And you're
right, no one thinks like that
anymore. Mostly because we've
been conditioned by the agenda of
the *modern woman*. Well-- just
because *we* decided to think and
act differently doesn't change the
facts.

Chapter 2

The Proper Environment

Everything created has a creator.
Wouldn't you agree? Would you
also agree that the thing created
was created to operate under
certain conditions? Would it be
feasible then, to think that the
thing's creator also designed an
ideal environment in order for the
thing to operate properly? If you
agree, then it would also be
reasonable to believe that the
creator would give instructions so
that the thing could function
properly.

Then wouldn't it make sense that
the instructions for the thing
would need to be followed in
order for the thing to function
properly?

For example, cars have a creator,
right? Now you wouldn't expect
a car to run if the instructions say
put the key in and turn it and you
put the key in but you don't turn
it...right? And you wouldn't
expect that car to operate properly
if the instructions say drive it on
dry land and instead you attempt
to drive it underwater. . . would
you?

Let's look at another example.
Let's say a child gets his first pet,
a goldfish. The instructions say,
keep the fish in clean water and
feed it fish food once a day. Now
the child loves his new pet but it's
so small and it can't go to the
park and play with him. The
child wants the fish to grow big
and become his playmate. So he
decides to take the fish out of its

water environment, take him to the park and feed him chopped vegetables 3 times a day to help the fish grow big and strong. After all, that's what *he* does to grow big and strong. Is that child going to get the results he wants? He meant well, he loved his pet, but because he did not follow the instructions on how to care for the pet, he got the exact opposite of what he wanted to achieve.

Let's recap: the instructions on how to care for the pet were not followed and it was taken out of its ideal environment which eventually led to its demise. Umm . . . let's think about that for a moment!!!

Everything created has a set of instructions and an ideal environment in which to function properly. Men and women are no exception. Before creating us, our creator provided an ideal environment and some instructions for us to follow in order for us to function properly.

For generations before us, men and women followed the instructions created specifically for each gender, and maintained their respective environments. It was a simpler time; men and women were not confused about their roles.

If today's woman is any indication, it must have been awful for her back then, as she has reinvented herself today and has made a complete 180 degree turn from the role that was intended for her by her creator. If you think about it, that assumes that the thing created is actually smarter than its creator. But wait! Is that even possible?

Umm . . . something else to think about...*Ladies!*

Even if not always perfect, there is something to be said about a life without the everyday stresses of maintaining "Super Mom" status or the pressure of climbing corporate ladders and breaking through class ceilings. There's even more to be said about a *healthy, fulfilling love-life.*

What if-- you actually had time to raise and care for your children . . . *yourself!*

What if-- you actually had enough energy at the end of the day to look forward to planning romantic adventures for you and your mate to enjoy on a regular basis?

What if --you weren't constantly struggling in one way or another to run a household that clearly requires two people, playing two *different* roles?

The point is there are certain things that must be done in order for us to achieve the things we *say* we want. It is as simple as that. And yet, we, intelligent women continue to operate a certain way. Our way. We are living our lives – not according to our creator's original instructions – but as we see fit, and yet we somehow expect an outcome that is only achieved through the instructions we ignore.

As well, we expect to live happily ever after in an environment that was not intended for us. The reality is that some things are not a gray area. Some things really are black and white, and no amount of playing *superwoman* or maintaining a 'having it all' mentality is going to change that. If we were really smart, we would embrace our womanhood and all that comes with it. We might just discover that we could be happy and content and fulfilled beyond our wildest dreams. Did you ever want something so badly; something that was really good for you, and what you got instead was something *far better* than anything you could have imagined for yourself?

Well . . . it's like that! It's called **automatic success**. It's the thing that just happens. We don't have to *strive* for it. We don't have to figure it out or strategically plan it. All we have to do to attain it is follow our *original designer's instructions on womanhood.*

Ok! Let's recap . . . and Ladies, really think about it!

Everything created has a creator. The creator provides instructions for the thing created to follow in order for it to operate properly. The creator also designed an ideal environment in order for the thing created to function properly.

Here is an exercise to help comprehend this point:

EXERCISE:

Match the ideal environment to the following things:

Things	Ideal Environment
boat	dirt
men	dry land
grass	a stable home
women	a lake
car	2 parent home
whale	a happy home
child	a cool room
computer	an ocean

When a thing is taken out of its ideal environment, it doesn't function properly. Too many of us women are functioning outside of our ideal environment. Our creator developed a perfect environment for us and we have all but left it behind to find something "*better*" because we're so smart and independent. We think happiness and fulfillment awaits us in other environments.

Ones that were never intended for us. Mainly, the environment our creator designed for the ruler of the world – *Man*! Now—about those instructions…

What are these so-called instructions? And why do we need them? *Instructions are procedures and guidelines provided by a creator or manufacturer in order for the creation to work and function properly.*

If we continue to follow society's changing and shifting instructions, we will continue to get society's results. But if we follow the instructions of our original "manufacturer," we will achieve automatic success. Meaning, we could have happiness, fulfillment and contentment (all the things we women claim to be striving for) automatically. Wow! How simple.

For example:

When a seed is in its proper environment, it will grow . . . *automatically*!

When a child is in the proper environment, he will flourish . . . *automatically!*

When a woman is in her proper environment, she is *automatically* 'womanly'. And...desired by men.

When a man is in his proper environment, he *automatically* thrives and there is nothing he can't achieve!

Remember, when men thrive, women reap the benefits. Ladies, let's help them thrive.

When we don't follow our original creator's instructions, we don't operate properly, then we begin to malfunction and eventually break down. It really is as simple as that.

In order to be the best woman you can be, you must operate in the proper environment. Not one where there is no healthcare for the babies. Not one where there is barely a roof over your heads. Not one where there are no funds in the bank. Not one where there is not enough food in the cupboards. Not one where there are creditors calling daily. Not one where you are utterly exhausted on a daily basis. Women were not designed to operate in those types of environments. And as a result, we *can't* function properly in those types of environments.

Just think about it for a moment, what would life be like if you didn't have to contend with those things? What better ways could you spend your time? Maybe you could actually be *present* for your child(ren) and/or your mate for a change. Then you really would be a *great catch*. Just think about it . . . And while you're thinking about that . . . think about this . . .

In order for a man to be the best he can be, he *must* be able to operate in *his* proper environment. Not one where he has to fight for what he is naturally entitled to. Yes, I said it. He is entitled to – as **the ruler of the world** – *sex, dinner, peace, cleanliness and a sexy sight!* That really is all it takes to keep him happy and satisfied...and when he's happy and satisfied guess where you'll be---right up there on top of that pedestal where you rightfully belong . . . *happy and satisfied too!*

It really is as simple as that, Ladies! In order to achieve true happiness and fulfillment beyond your wildest imagination, just follow the simple instructions given by your original creator and you will begin to reap the benefits of womanhood.

Don't be duped by modern society. Remember, in any household, there can only be one head. There are no exceptions.

No substitutes. There is no such thing as a 50/50 relationship and there is certainly nothing equal about men and women.

Men are naturally stronger--we are the weaker vessel; men are naturally more practical--we are more emotional; men are natural conquerors, their instincts are to conqueror it in order to get it-- a woman's instinct is to nurture it in order to make it right, as we are natural nurturers. Men are not wired to be emotional or nurturing, yet we keep expecting to find these characteristics in our men. When we don't, we try to condition them to be. Then when we succeed, we complain that they are weak. Ladies, just ***Stop It!*** Allow them to be who they naturally are.

The fact is, all of our natural, but different characteristics work for the good of both men and women when we operate in harmony. The characteristics in men, *balance* out women and vice versa.

However, *balance* does not mean equal. B*alance* is *equilibrium*. According to Webster's, *equality* means – *the quality of being equal. Quality – a degree of excellence*.

Instead of spinning our wheels, trying to be equal to men, maybe *balance* is the key to a *quality* existence between the sexes.

What is balance? And how do we achieve it? Webster's says – *balance is to bring into harmony or proportion.* To achieve it, we simply do our part and *let* men do their part. Not exactly rocket science . . .uhh?

It never was. We tend to make things much harder than they really are. As human beings, we conjure up things to be more complicated than they are. Why? Probably because we want to elevate ourselves above others.

We all have a natural desire to do that on some level. The truth is, these situations and dilemmas, we make out to be so complicated are really not complicated at all. In fact they're pretty simple, and there are usually simple solutions. I taught my children from a very young age that every problem has a solution. No exceptions! As a result, they approach everything with a "can do" attitude. Maybe today's *modern women* should try this 'can do' approach to become *real women.* Yes, there really is a solution to every single problem on the planet!!! Sometimes there's more than one solution and most times, the solution is simple.

The point is, the answer to the mystery of men vs. women is right in front of us and is not really a mystery at all.

We can keep telling ourselves that things have changed, but that won't change the facts, and the facts are that the original instructions for men and women are still in **full effect**. I know it's hard to imagine that in today's high-tech world, no one has come up with a *better* way.

But wait!!!

Maybe . . . just maybe . . . this is the best way. Have we ever stopped to think that maybe **our creator, created the very best for us** and all we have to do is accept that fact and reap the benefits? Maybe the original instructions that were designed specifically for men and women and their relationships were not just some half-cocked ideas. Maybe this whole man/women concept was very well planned and thought out even beyond our comprehension. Maybe every little detail of our instructions has a purpose, and every part of those instructions is there for a reason . . . an important reason. Maybe this is the case . . . even though we can't see it or understand it. If only we could get out of our own way and just go with it. For some reason, women seem to have a harder time accepting things as they were designed than men do. Men seem fine not to change a thing. While women seem to want to change everything. Why is that? Is it because we think men got the better deal? Maybe they did or maybe not, but even if that were true . . . so what? Let them! After all . . . it's <u>their</u> world . . . remember?

And also—even if it were true, what are we going to do? We can't change it. We can continue to try but we won't prevail. The good news is, maybe we weren't meant to be privy to all the details of how the universe works, and maybe it all works out for the best, anyway . . . if we let it.

If we women would readily accept our role as women, we would automatically reap the rewards . . . and benefits of womanhood. Not by demanding or fighting for what we *think* we want. Not by going after what we want, when we want it and by any means necessary, but by embracing the "special-order item" we were specifically designed to be *by our creator.* It is as simple as that!

Chapter 3
Purpose

Let's take a look at an incubator.
Incubators do not originate
anything. An incubator takes
things in, grows them, develops
them, multiplies them, and then
gives them back.

Whatever is put into an incubator
comes back *ready, better,
improved and/or multiplied.*
Women are natural incubators.

It's been said that if you give a
woman a house, she'll give you a
home. If you give her food, she'll
give you a meal. If you give her a
seed, she'll give you a life.

You can only get something from an incubator if you put something in. Hold on to this thought—for it will come up again.

If we as women go back to being what our creator created us to be, we would achieve automatic success and happiness beyond anything we could imagine for ourselves. We spend a lot of time trying to figure out things that have already been figured out for us, like how to get the things we naturally crave. Things like— protection—security-- and strength. We women naturally want to feel protected. We also want to feel secure.

Strength, be it mental or physical, is something we sometimes need more of than we have. And from time to time, we will need more strength than we are physically capable of providing for ourselves. We sometimes need muscle – male muscle – and all the *working out* in the world will

not do the trick. Let's face it
Ladies . . . *we need men*! They
and only they can provide the
kind of protection—security—and
strength that we naturally crave.

They are the inventors, the
originators of things. We are the
incubators that grow, develop and
multiply the things that men
originate.

<u>They</u> are our strength, our
protectors and our security. But--
it's a package deal, Ladies! And
we must accept the pros and the
cons of it. All of it!

After all, we are the incubators of
our children. Remember what we
said about, getting out of an
incubator, what we put in…

It's time to accept our true role!!!

Chapter 4

It's A Man's World!

It's a man's world? Really? A
man's world? So where does that
leave us women? Isn't it our
world too? Shouldn't we be
sharing the world? Aren't we
equal now? 50/50? Better yet--
why can't it just be our world?
After all, women seem to be in
charge of everything anyway.
Men don't seem to be stepping
up. Someone has to take charge.
It might as well be us women,
right?

Wrong!

In fact, we need to just chill,
relax, back up, step back and give
men their world back. And while
we're at it--let's give them back
all of their belongings: their
workplaces-- their voices-- their
manhood!!!

After all, we took all of *their* stuff
and abandoned all of our own
stuff. Now we're all confused--
about everything, what to do--
how to do it-- when to do it-- who
should do it. We have blurred the
gender roles severely and now we
must face the fact that it is time to
<u>give men their world back</u>. It's
time for men to take their rightful
place in the world: RULER,
LEADER, MASTER. Then we
can all get back on track.

Yes! I know it's short—short and
sweet. You see, sometimes you
don't need all the long and drawn
out details. Sometimes you need--
Just the facts!

Chapter 5

Feminists:
Friend or Foe

Now before you jump on the
feminist bandwagon regarding the
whole 'man's world' issue, let me
point out a few facts that resulted
from women being in charge.
And by the way, why do we feel
the need to be in charge anyway?
Does it really make us happier? It
seems like today's woman is
actually less happy and more
stressed than women of the pre-
feminist movement. Why are
women seemingly so unhappy
with the course of their lives
today? After all, thanks to the

feminist movement, we got everything we said we wanted, right? We got equal rights, equal pay, 50/50 relationships. We can act like men, dress like men, have as much sex as men do, with as many partners. We got to have our freedom by buying our own homes, we got to take the jobs men used to have and save for our own retirement fund in case we want to (or have to) retire alone, we even got to have—and raise children without fathers because it was more convenient and less complicated for us . . . not so much for the children or the fathers, just for us—the women! So what is our problem? We got everything we said we wanted, right?

So why are we so unhappy, so discontented, and so unfulfilled?

Why?

I'll tell you why!

BECAUSE WE GOT EVERYTHING WE WANTED!

That's why!

The problem is,

EVERYTHING IS TOO MUCH!

EVERYTHING is more than we bargained for.

HAVING IT ALL, as it turns out is not all it was cracked up to be!

In fact, it is quite frankly, impossible to *really* have it all – physically impossible. So what we really got was a very stressful existence.

Now let's back up.

Generations ago, women were brought up and taught to understand the male ego. Women were also taught to work *with* the male disposition, not against it. A

49

young woman was taught how to properly use her femininity-- her womanly powers-- if you will. Yes, I said womanly powers (more on that later in the series).

Unfortunately lessons in "womanhood" no longer exist. The 60's came along and the women's liberation movement saw this as an unnecessary form of manipulation and set out to all but abolish the practice.

Back then, lots of young impressionable women jumped on the feminist bandwagon and thus began the *superwoman* era that we all are still feeling the effects of today. The real problem with the feminist movement was that the "feminine" part of the movement always seemed to be missing from the movement. The movement, instead, seem to only highlight all of the so-called burdens of being female. As a result, today's women are being brought up and taught to work

tirelessly to rid themselves of
these so-called burdens.

These include the burden of:
- having a uterus
- a monthly menstrual cycle
- pregnancy
- marriage
- virginity
- men as our leaders
- our children's fathers
- actually raising our own
children

Some of the practices being used
today to eliminate "female
burdens" are:

The burden	The elimination
a uterus	a hysterectomy
menstrual cycle	pills/patches
pregnancy	abortion
marriage	shacking up

virginity	promiscuity
men	wearing *the* pants
fathers	sperm banks
child rearing	nannies, daycare babysitters

These are things we can thank the feminist movement for. Was the feminist movement really our friend? Are we really benefiting from that whole thing?

News Flash. . . Ladies!
All of those so-called female burdens are actually womanly gifts. We should feel *privileged* to have them—not burdened.

Now fast forward to today's woman – the 21st Century Woman. We have it all together right?

Wrong!

Most young women today are automatic feminists because they were raised by mothers of the feminist era. They don't give a second thought to gender roles and womanhood. They've been re-programmed by society.

Even-though I was raised in the 60's, and in the heart of the movement, I was lucky enough to be raised by a mother who, for whatever reason, was *not* a feminist. My mother was a stay-at- home mom who obeyed (yes I said it) obeyed her husband, raised her five children *herself* and seemed pretty content with her life. She may not always have been content, but we, her children sure didn't see it. That gave my siblings and me a real sense of security growing up. Today, I thank her regularly for that childhood, for her gift of time, for teaching me by example, for teaching without preaching, and for being "all things lady-like." I

believe that the healthy childhood environment she provided is the reason I can see clearly today. That's not to say I did everything right. On the contrary,
I've made bad choices in just about every area of my life, which is another reason I can see so clearly today, what I couldn't see back then. If I could have a do-over, there are about a million and one things I would do differently. But, we don't get a do-over. That ship has sailed and we only have the present to make better choices. We cannot be prideful or embarrassed, for we are all human and there is no doubt that we have all made mistakes and will more than likely make more. The point is, *"when you know better, you do better!*

Now back to today's woman. As a result of being born into feminism, today's women don't seem to understand much about the male mindset, the male ego or the male disposition. We are convinced that men and women are the same. Oh, we won't admit it but our actions prove it every time we "make the first move", every time we move-in before marriage, every time we deny men the opportunity to be chivalrous. Deep down we don't believe men and women are wired differently. But, we've got to stop fooling ourselves and face reality. We expect our worldly actions to produce heavenly results. Oh we *can* achieve the results we're striving for, but it's going to take a change of mindset . . . *and principles.*

After all, you wouldn't go to school to study auto mechanics, then come out and expect to get a job as a brain surgeon, would you?

As well Ladies, we can't continue to go through life acting like men and expect to be treated like women. It just won't happen. Furthermore, we are confusing our men when we do this. They don't know when to do what.

And, until we change our mindset and our actions, the gender challenge will continue.

Are you up to the challenge?

Are you woman enough?!!!

The key is to think about the choices you make today because every choice you make, has a consequence – sometimes good and sometimes bad. And every choice you make *will* affect more than just yourself. It will affect those around you.

This is especially true for women. We need to consider that what *we* do and how we do it, may very well determine the outcome and/or future of the men in our lives as well as our children's lives.

Ladies we may not rule the world, but the quality of the world's future is in our hands.

To be continued . . .

It is my sincere hope, that women everywhere will read this series with an open heart and an open mind.

Miss Charlette

Genesis 2:18   *Matthew 19:9*

Deuteronomy 22:20-21

1Peter 3:1-2

Mark 10:11-12   Ephesians 5:33

Proverbs 31

When you know better,

1 Corinthians 11: 8-9

Ephesians 5: 25

Matthew 19:5   Ephesians 5:22-24

Genesis 3:16

You do better!

Deuteronomy 22:5

1Peter 3:7

1Corinthians 11:3-14

www.ingramcontent.com/pod-product-compliance
Lightning Source LLC
Chambersburg PA
CBHW060225290526
45789CB00003B/1420

* 9 7 8 1 4 6 6 2 6 2 6 6 9 *